CLASSICAL ROMANTIC ERA ART
COLORING BOOK
Volume 4
Classic Art Coloring Book Series

Drawings and text by Denise McGill

I0475754

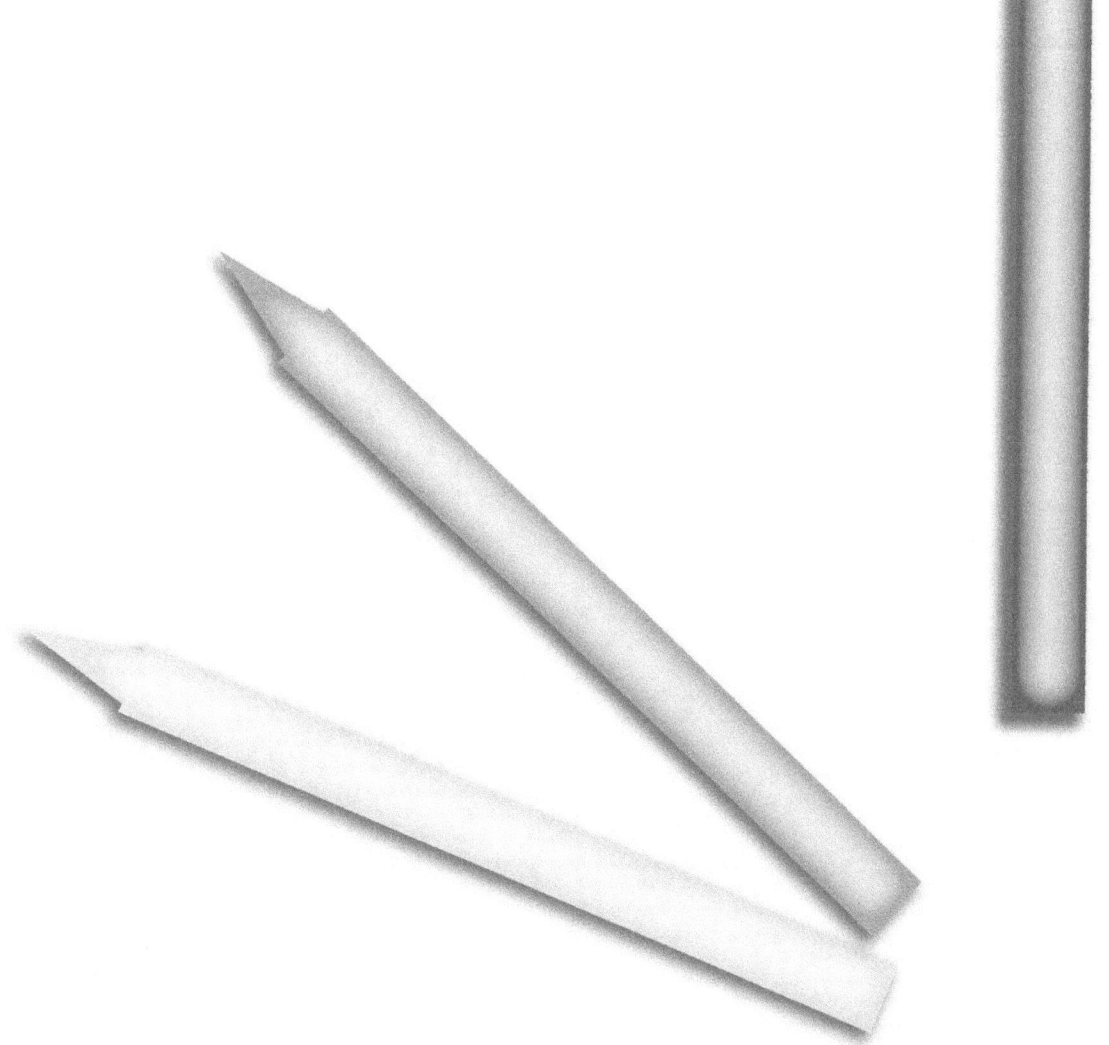

Text and illustration copyright 2007, 2013, by Denise McGill

All rights reserved. No part of this publication my be repro-
ducted or transmitted in any form or by any means, electronic
or mechanical including photocopy, recording, or any informa-
tion torage and retrieval system, all or in part except for the
classroom use or individual projects or by the express permis-
sion of the author.

Classical Romantic Era Art Coloring Book

Table of Contents

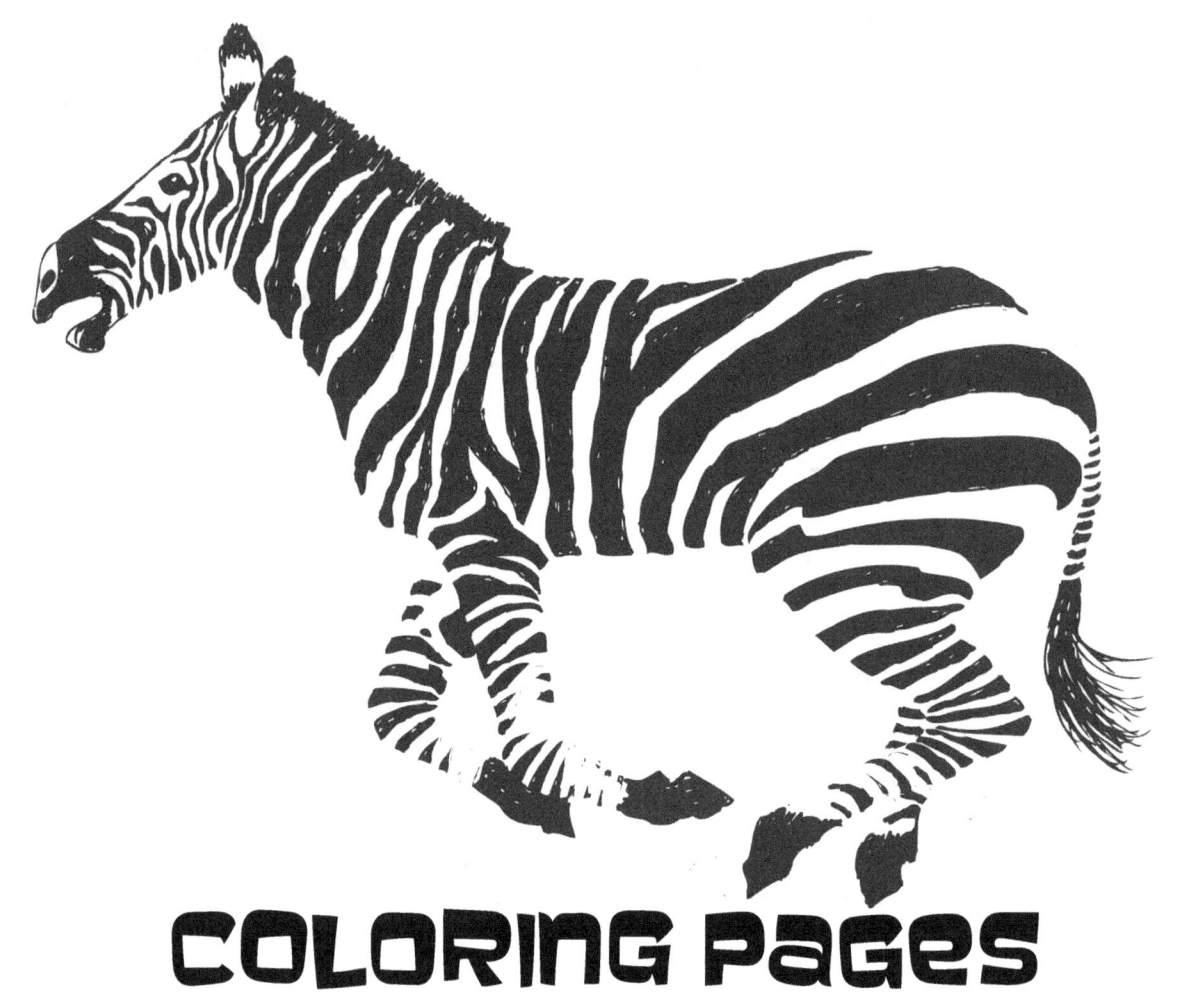

COLORING PAGES

As simplistic as it may seem, coloring the art of a renowned artist is an excellent method of introducing art to students. They see the work and recognize it. They may not be able to name the artist and year just by having colored the piece, but they will always remember it. To add more to the learning experience, it is suggested that you check out a library book on each artist or go online and look up the work of art after allowing the children to color it their way. Then seeing how the artist painted the piece, what colors were used how large or small the finished piece was, helps enforce the learning experience. It is up to each educator to decide on whether to check out the art before the students color the page or after. If they see the piece before they color theirs, they may be influence to copy, or use the same colors the artist did. If they see the piece after, they may be surprised at the color choice of the artist and even pleased with their own choices.

after the Renaissance

Mannerism

Closely following the Renaissance was the Mannerism movement where artists chose to escape the rigid faithfulness of nature and elongate and distort the human figure, using vivid colors for impact. Although many thought El Greco may have had vision problems, he was one of the best remembered of this movement.

Baroque Art

From 1600 through around 1750 is a period in art known as the Baroque period. This is when emotions were clearly added to the scientific observation of the Renaissance. Many painters clearly kept

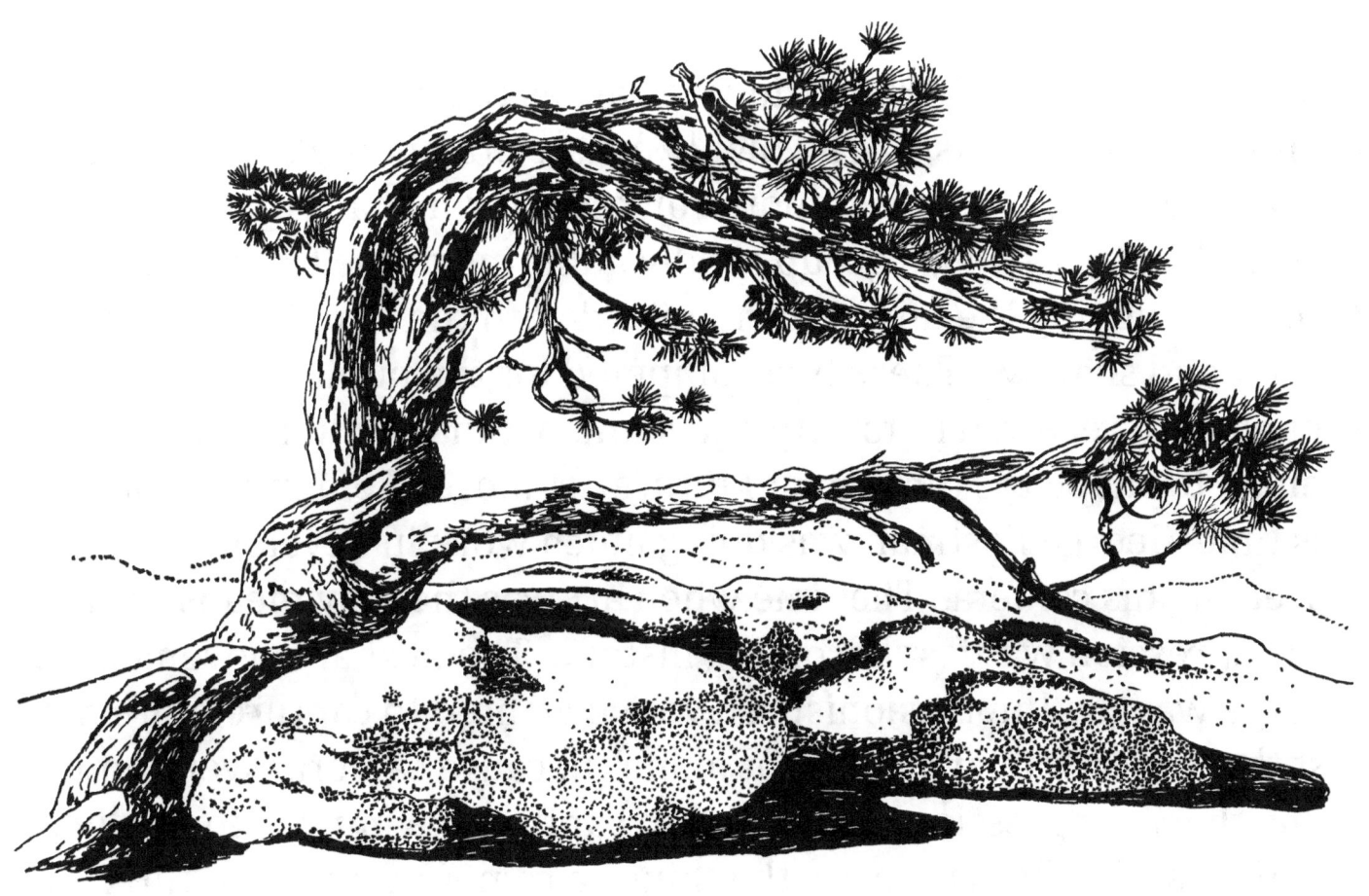

religious themes, even those of different faiths, throughout this period. There was an ornate decorative quality to the paintings of this period and plenty of romance. In the area of music, this period is known as the Romantic period.

Rococo Art

From about 1700 through 1750 is known as the Rococo period in art. This took the decorative quality and went a step further into the overly ornate. One commentator suggested they took the "feast for the eyes" into down right gluttony. The Rococo period was not limited to art but also architecture, furniture, carriages, and clothing. Everything was taken over the top in ornate flourishes. Many are happy this was a short-lived period. Paper Mache became popular, as it could be used on walls and doors to add flourishes and swirls everywhere.

Romanticism and Neoclassicism

From about 1750 to 1880 is known in art as the period of Romanticism and Neo-classicism. The highly ornate era of the Baroque and Rococo gave way to a looser more romantic form of art, on one hand; and on the other hand, a group rigidly adhering to the Greek classical forms of studying the human form mixed with the Renaissance study of light and shadow. These two competed for the public approval and though both received notoriety and some popularity, Romanticism seemed to shape the direction of future art more. Remember about this time, George Eastman was doing much work in developing and perfecting his camera. The time when art was the only means of visual expression was fast becoming history. The next art movement to emerge was the Impressionist art, which wanted to capture more than just the perfect camera snapshot of life (because cameras were now doing that). Impressionists wanted to capture the impression of life, emotion, and light. These are the things a camera cannot capture.

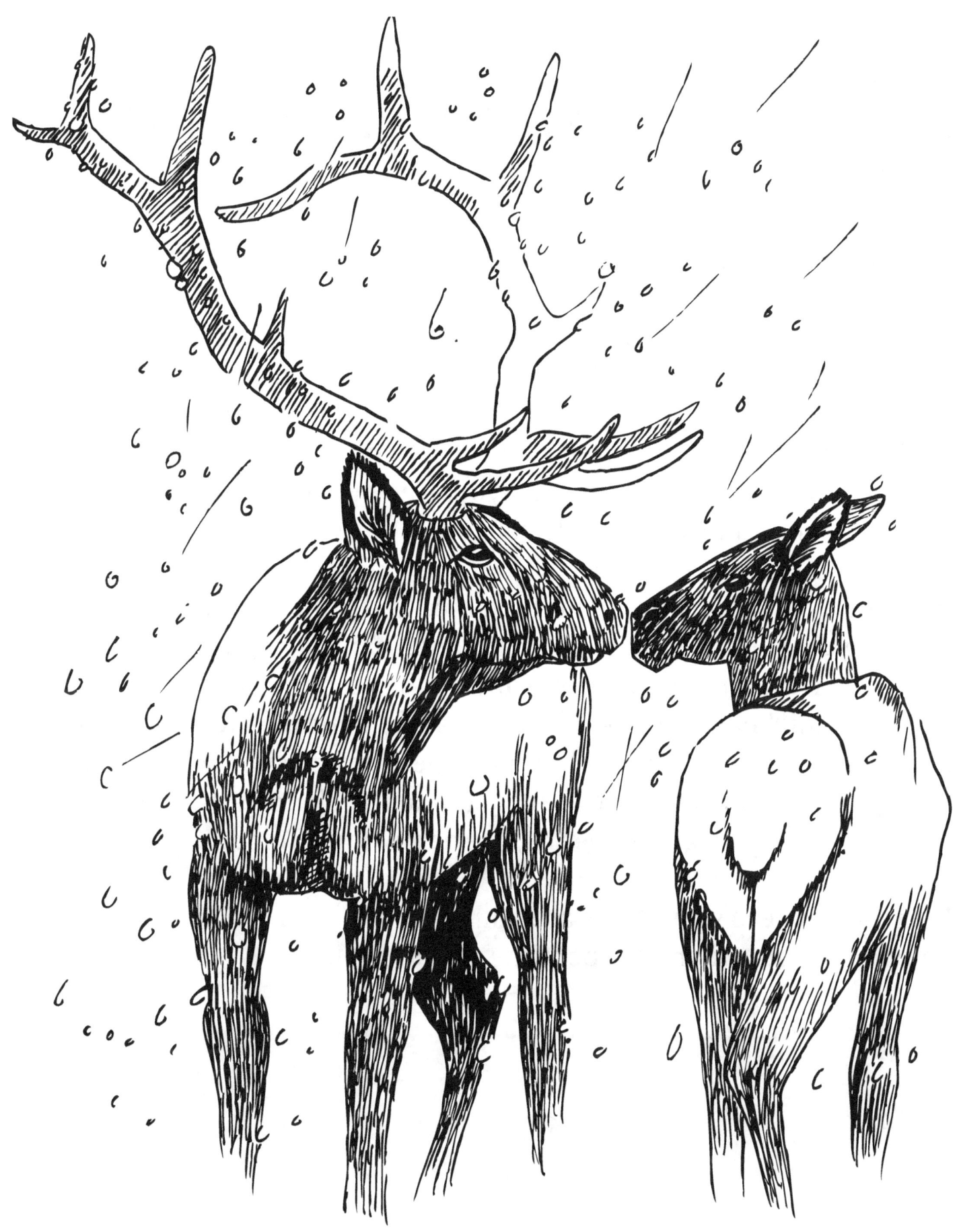

eL GReCO (DOMeNIKOS THeOTOKOPOULOUS), 1541-1614

Portrait of Brother Hortensio Paravicino, 1609

Although El Greco was of Greek origin, he relocated and made his home in Spain, greeting influencing the Spanish Renaissance and many art movements beyond. His style of elongating the faces and necks of his figures suggested to many art history students that he may have suffered from a visual myopathy. Whatever the reason, his work was charming and deeply religious.

In his early 20's, El Greco went to Venice and studied under Titian, learning the fundamentals of Renaissance painting and narrative painting. He later went to Rome and as the story goes, reportedly criticized Michelangelo's work, which some believe is why he left for Spain. He arrived in Madrid hoping to get commission work from King Phillip II but to no avail. He found a home in Toledo getting commission work from Diego de Castilla, the dean of the Toledo Cathedral.

Many of El Greco's paintings are still in churches in the little town of Toledo in Spain where he spent the rest of his life.

PORTRAIT OF BROTHER HORTENSIO PARAVICINO

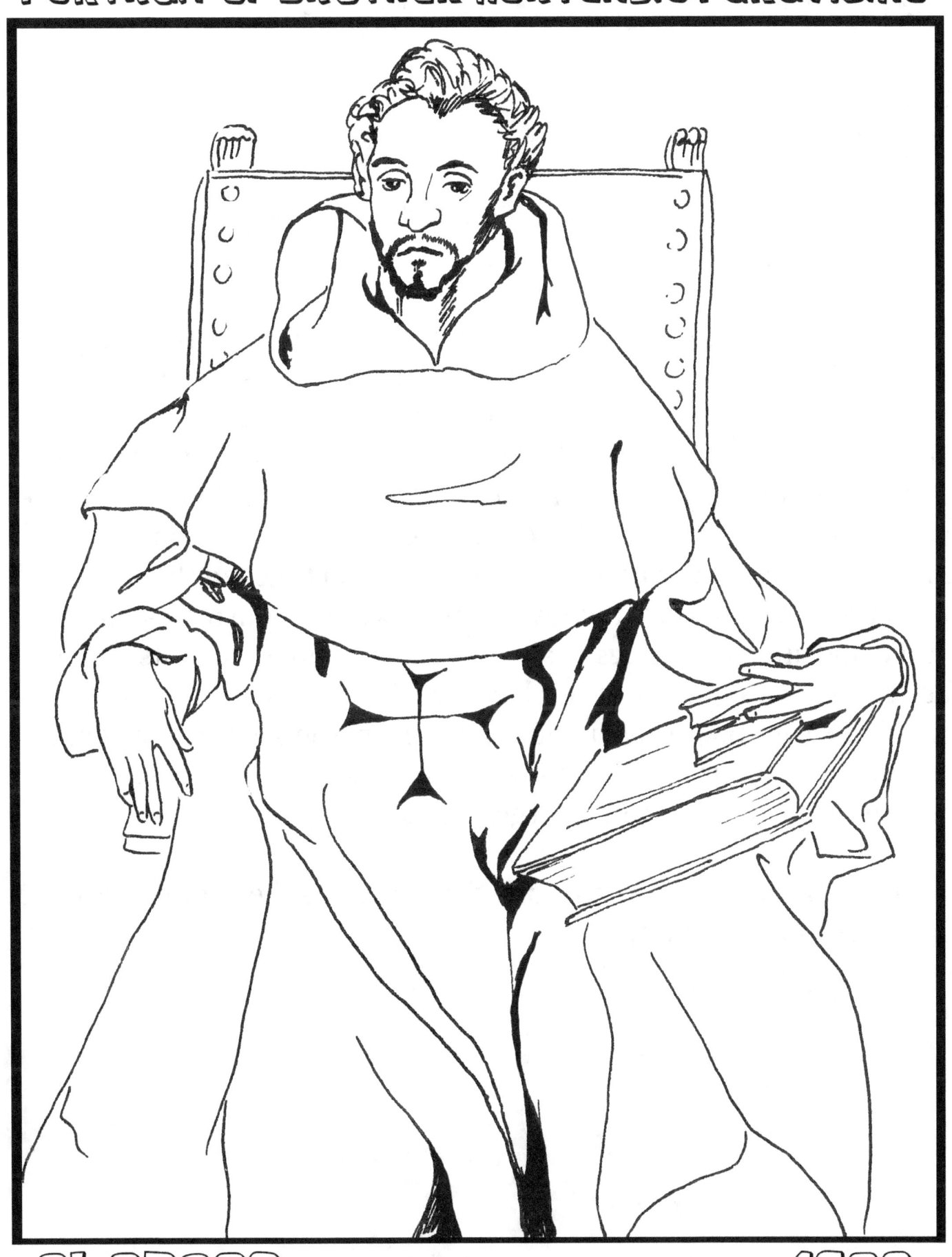

EL GRECO

1609

GeORGes De La TOUR, 1593-1652

The Newborn Child, 1630
Oil on canvas

A Frenchman who copied the "luminism" of Caravaggio, he painted with sharp contrasts of light and dark.

Georges, the second born of 7, grew up in well-to-do surroundings with many artisans as relatives. He was exposed to art at an early age. It is not known where he studied or if he apprenticed under an artist, but by the time he was in his early 20's and married, the Duke of Lorraine was buying some of his paintings. After the Duke died there was much upheaval among European monarchs for the domination of Lorraine. Because of this war and plague often touched the La Tour household. At one point the town was sacked and burnt, leaving his studio and all his paintings in ashes. This probably accounts for the fact that so few of his paintings have survived. At one point, he was called to Paris and received 1000 francs from the king for "services rendered." Although no one knows what service he rendered, he was referred to after that as Sir Georges de La Tour.

It is because of artists like this one that we know the common dress of the times in which they lived.

THE NEWBORN CHILD

GEORGES DE LATOUR

1630

Georges De LaTour, 1593-1652

The Old Man, 1625-27
Oil on canvas

Georges, the second born of 7, grew up in well-to-do surroundings with many artisans as relatives, although his father was a mason. He was exposed to art at an early age. It is not known where he studied or if he apprenticed under an artist, but by the time he was in his early 20's and married, the Duke of Lorraine was buying some of his paintings. After the Duke died there was much upheaval among European monarchs for the domination of Lorraine. Because of this war and plague often touched the La Tour household. At one point the town was sacked and burnt, leaving his studio and all his paintings in ashes. This probably accounts for the fact that so few of his paintings have survived. At one point, he was called to Paris and received 1000 francs from the king for "services rendered." Although no one knows what service he rendered, he was referred to after that as Sir Georges de La Tour.

Most of the works by La Tour are dated after 1640 because of the war and plague that the region went through, however a few pieces survived, such as this one. The painting is marked by the strong light and shadow contrast typical of La Tour's work. This fascination with lighting effects made him very popular in his lifetime but his fame faded after his death, only to be rediscovered again in modern times. This is typical of many artists and their works, falling in and out of popularity and discovery with the changing of generations.

THE OLD MAN

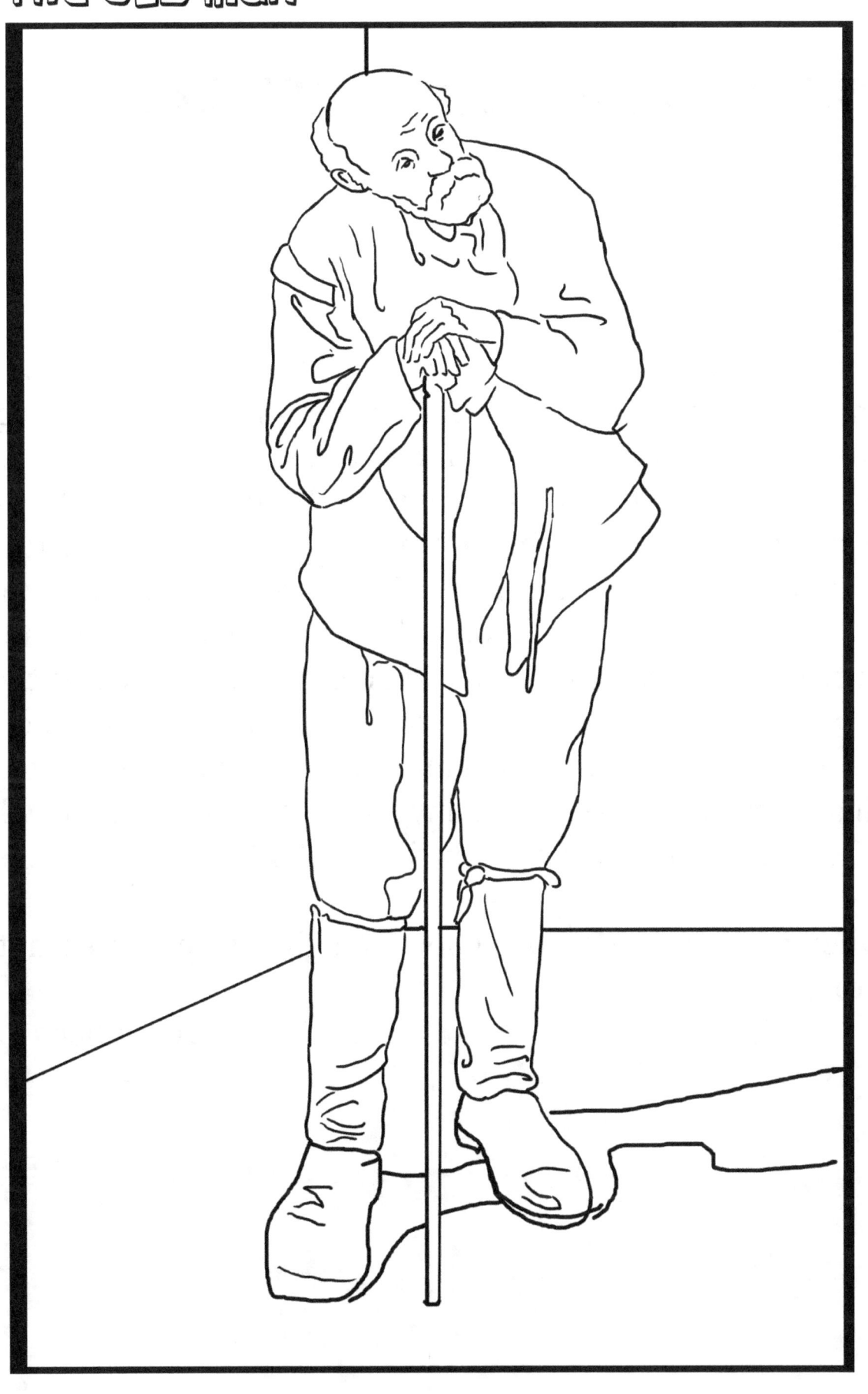

GEORGES DE LATOUR 1625-27

PETER PAUL RUBENS, 1577-1640

Night Scene, 1616-1617

Oil on Panel

Rubens was a Flemish Baroque painter well known for his Counter-Reformation alterpieces and his history paintings. He was knighted by both, Phillip IV, King of Spain and Charles I, King of England. Much of Rubens early artistic education involved copying works by earlier artists including Han Holbein the Younger and Raphael. He traveled to Italy to copy works by Titian and Tintoretto. In his many travels, he became both artist and diplomat between Spain and England, Italy and Antwerp. He was one of the last artists to use panels as the support for his paintings, even large works, although he also used canvas. He was a prolific painter, leaving many mythological and religious paintings to posterity. He had many students and assistants who became famous in their own right, including Anthony van Dyck.

"Sir, when their backsides look good enough to slap, there's nothing more to do."

Peter Paul Rubens

NIGHT SCENE

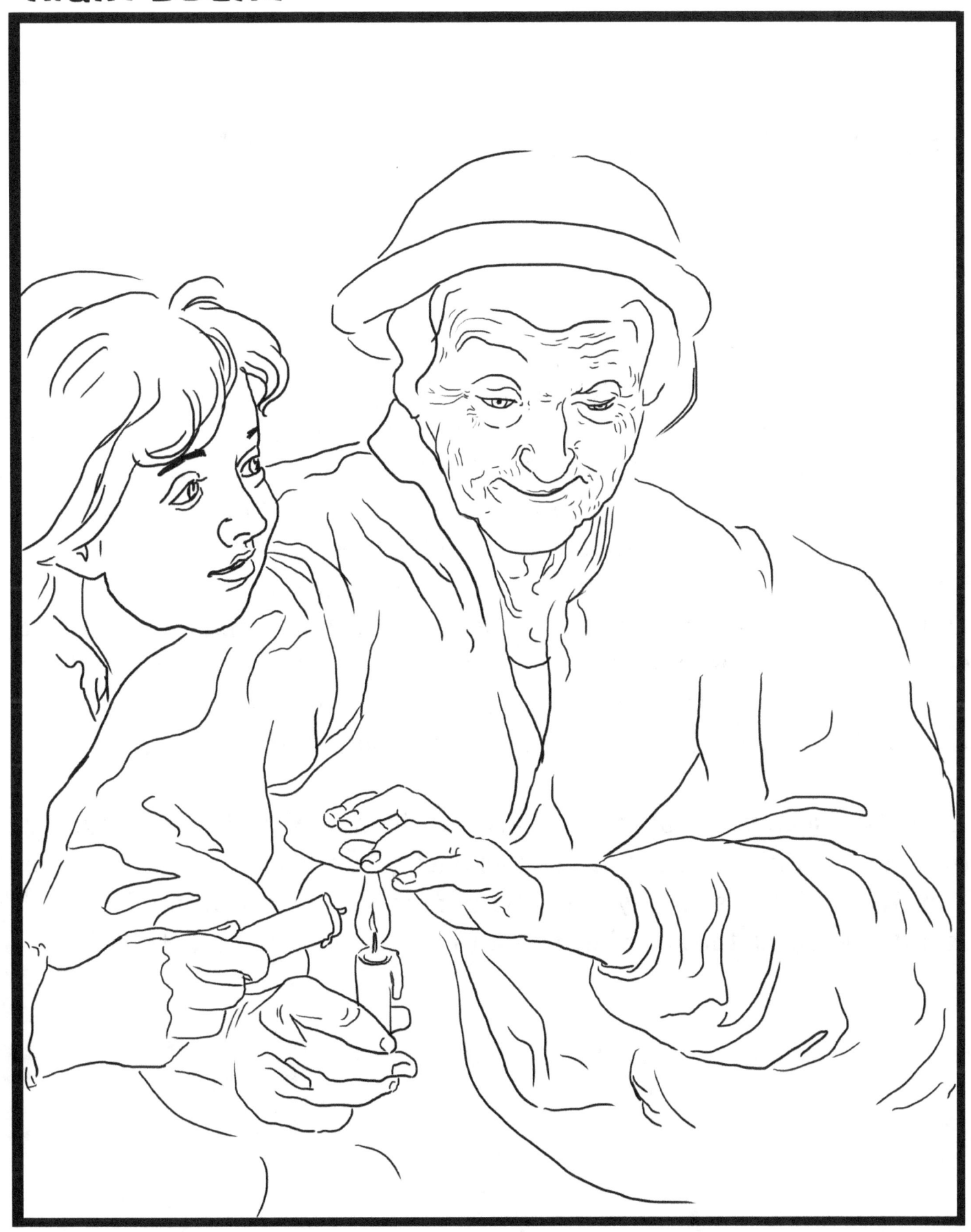

PETER PAUL RUBENS   1616-1617

SIR ANTOON VAN DYCK, 1599-1641

Portrait of Mary Ruthven, wife of the artist, 1635
Oil on Canvas

Van Dyck was an important Flemish Baroque painter, who influenced many other artists. He became the leading court painter in England under King James I and Charles I. He painted both portraits as well as biblical and mythological subjects. He was considered a an outstanding draftsman and innovator in watercolor and etching. In his early years he was the chief assistant under Peter Paul Rubens and was referred to as the best of his pupils. He was hugely popular in England and tended to "flatter" the royalty he painted, smoothing out teeth and skin, plumping where plumping was needed and thinning where thinning was needed. Many artists are taught to take 10 pound or so off a woman in painting them so that they will make their client happy.

A few landscapes in watercolor have survived by Van Dyke but mostly they were studies to be later used as backgrounds for portraits. Since Van Dyck painted so many portraits of men with short pointy beards, mainly Charles I, the style became known, especially in the US, as a

PORTRAIT OF MARY RUTHVEN, WIFE OF THE ARTIST

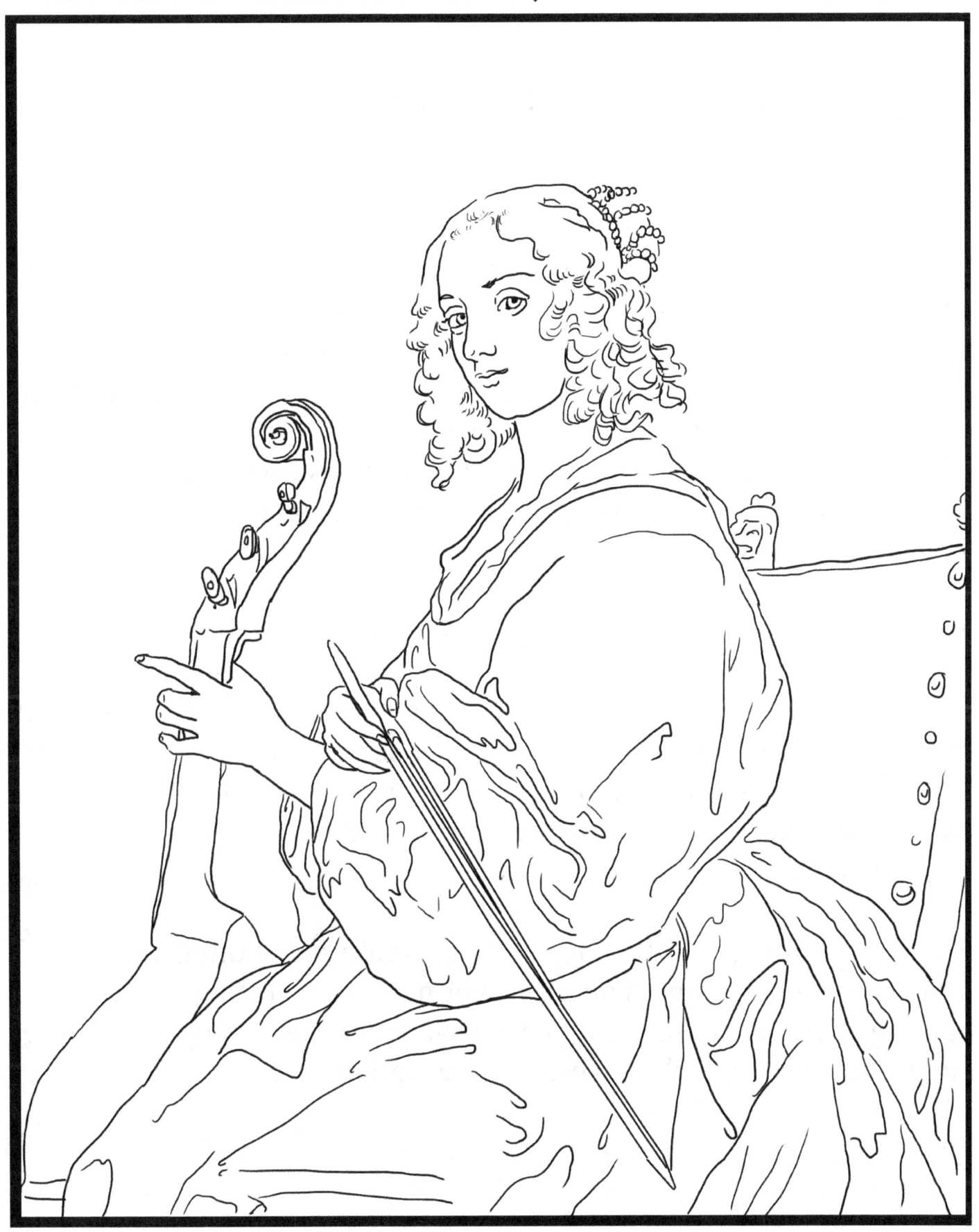

SIR ANTOON VAN DYCK   1635

vandyck beard.

REMBRANDT VAN RIJN, 1606-1669

Man in Armor, 1655

The Dutch painter, Rembrandt, started his career apprenticing under a then famous painter of historical paintings and after 6 months returned home to begin his own work. He became so highly regarded that he began taking on pupils by the age of 22. Although he had many commissions, he was famous as a teacher and his studio was often filled with pupils, some of which were already established artists. He married the cousin of an established art dealer, which greatly advanced his career.

Rembrandt was poor at managing money. He had a reputation for ostentatious living. When he was paid for a commissioned painting, he would often buy things he wanted instead of paying his bills. This suit of armor is something he wanted to paint so he bought it. By the time he died he was penniless and everything he owned had to be sold to pay for his funeral. The suit of armor was sold for a fraction of what he paid for it.

Although running out of money was disappointing, it often spurred him to create more works of art, sometimes exaggerating the stark lighting effects because darker colors were cheaper to buy than lighter and brighter ones, such as white, yellow and orange.

man in armor

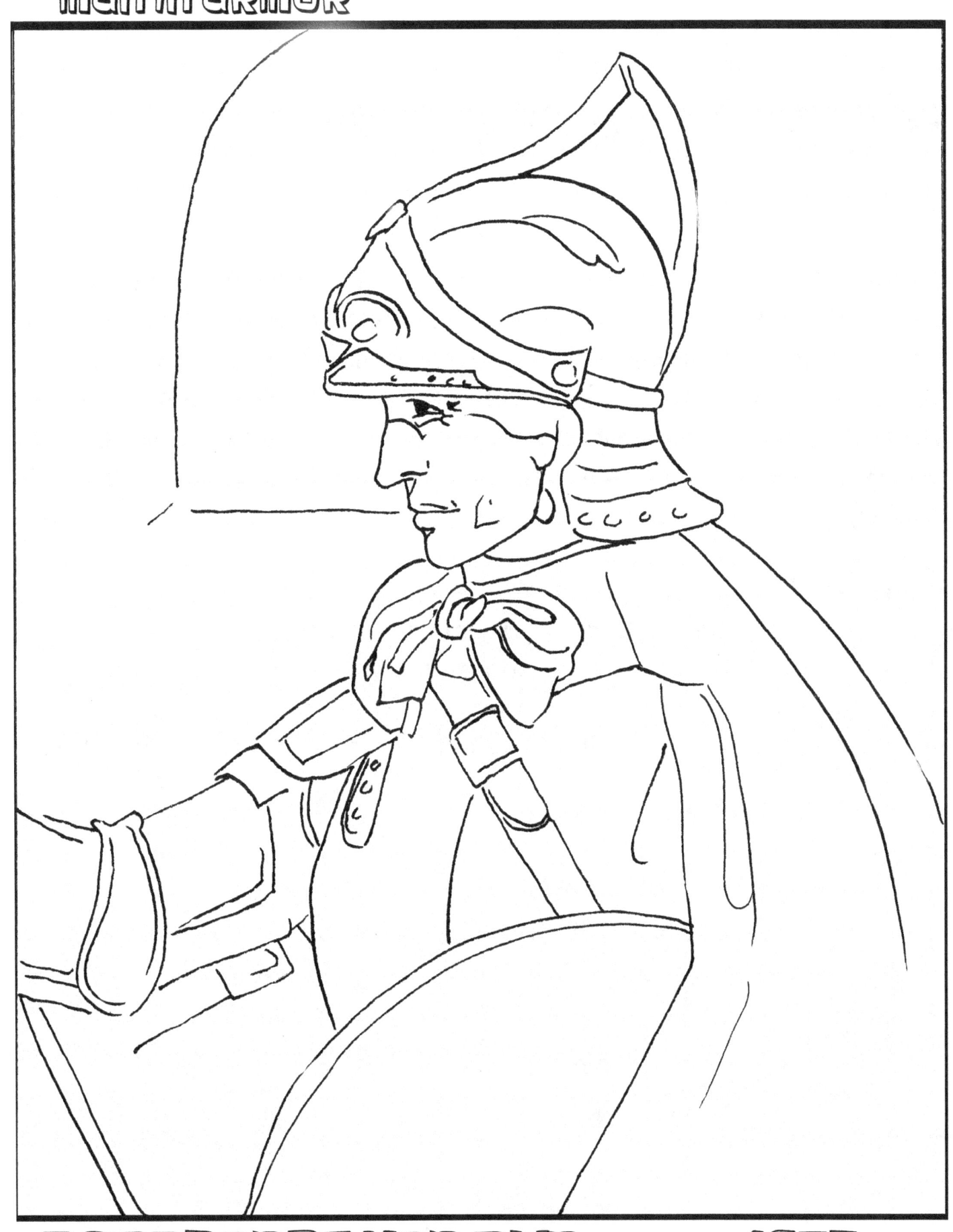

rembrandt van rijn   1655

Rembrandt Van Rijn, 1606-1669

Self-Portrait, 1666

Rembrandt is famous for painting in a way that looks like a window was just opened and light is shining only on the subject, with the rest of the picture in darkness. The real reason for this is because dark colors such as brown and black were cheaper, and rich colors such as white, yellow and red were much more expensive. Perhaps his great style was born out of the necessity to conserve the more expensive paints.

At any rate, his life was marred with tragedy, when his wife and 3 children died. Only the last born, Titus, survived. His housekeeper and nurse to Titus, later became his common law wife and model for many of his later works. When his common law wife died and Titus, at the age of 27, died, the artist fell into grief and died just 11 months later.

SELF-PORTRAIT

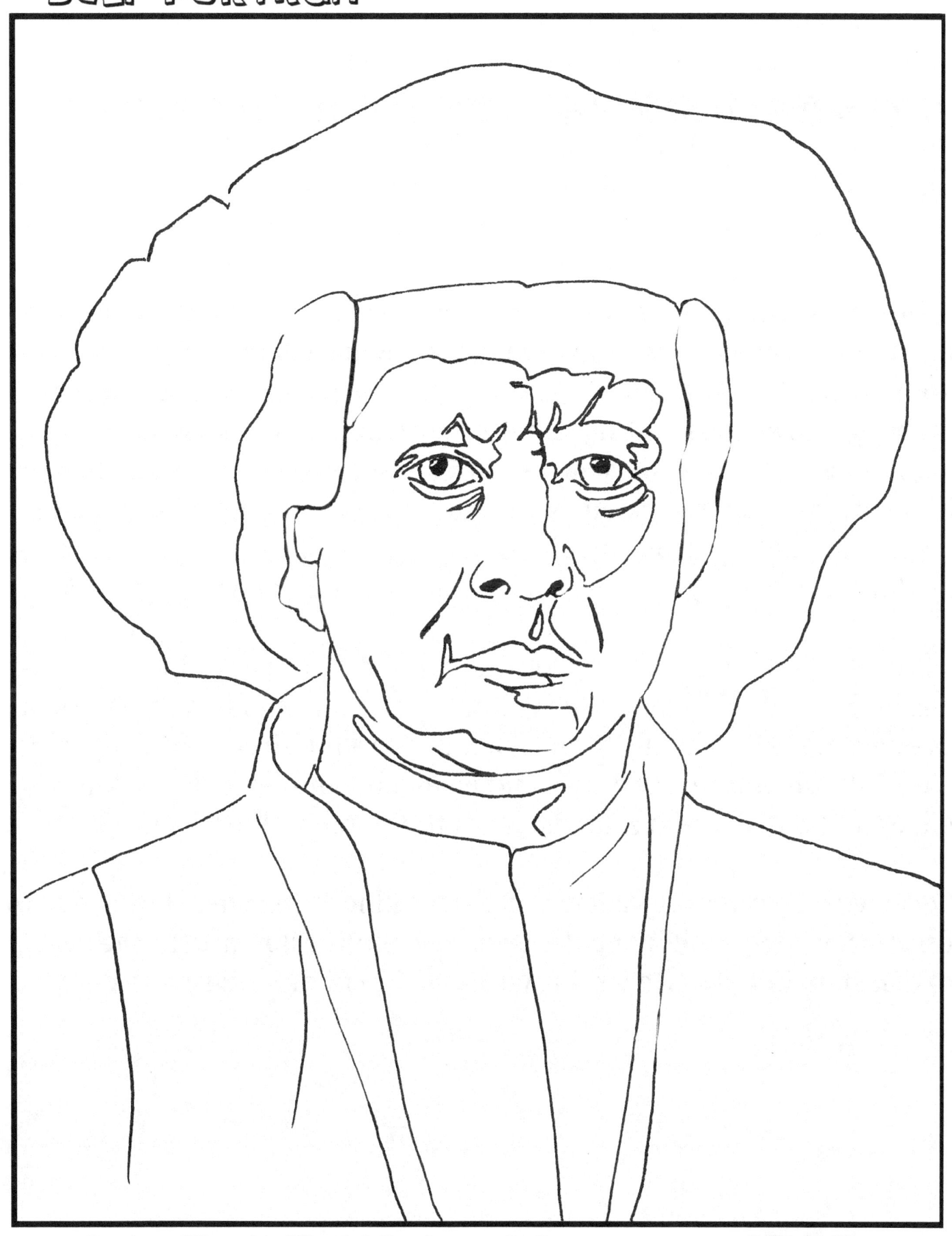

REMBRANDT VAN RIJN   1666

Jan Vermeer van Delft, 1632-1675

The Cook, 1660
Oil on canvas

A Dutch Baroque painter like Rembrandt, Vermeer is famous for painting indoor scenes of everyday life in the town of Delft. Very little is known about his life and his way of painting. He would take up to 6 months on a single painting and therefore he did not make money very quickly. Some believe he used the first camera obscura to help him with perspective. Some believe because he left his wife and children in debt at his death that he was not particularly popular, however he did receive many commissions and painted extraordinary works.

His capture of the common people and their work has helped historians and fashion designers throughout the years establish the dress of the day. He was virtually forgotten for over a hundred years but came back into the interest of critics and is hugely popular today, acknowledges and one of the great masters of the Dutch Golden Age.

Vermeer died after only a day and half of illness, his wife stated, due to financial stresses following the severe economic downturn (the year of disaster) in Delft. He left his wife and 11 children in severe debt.

THE COOK

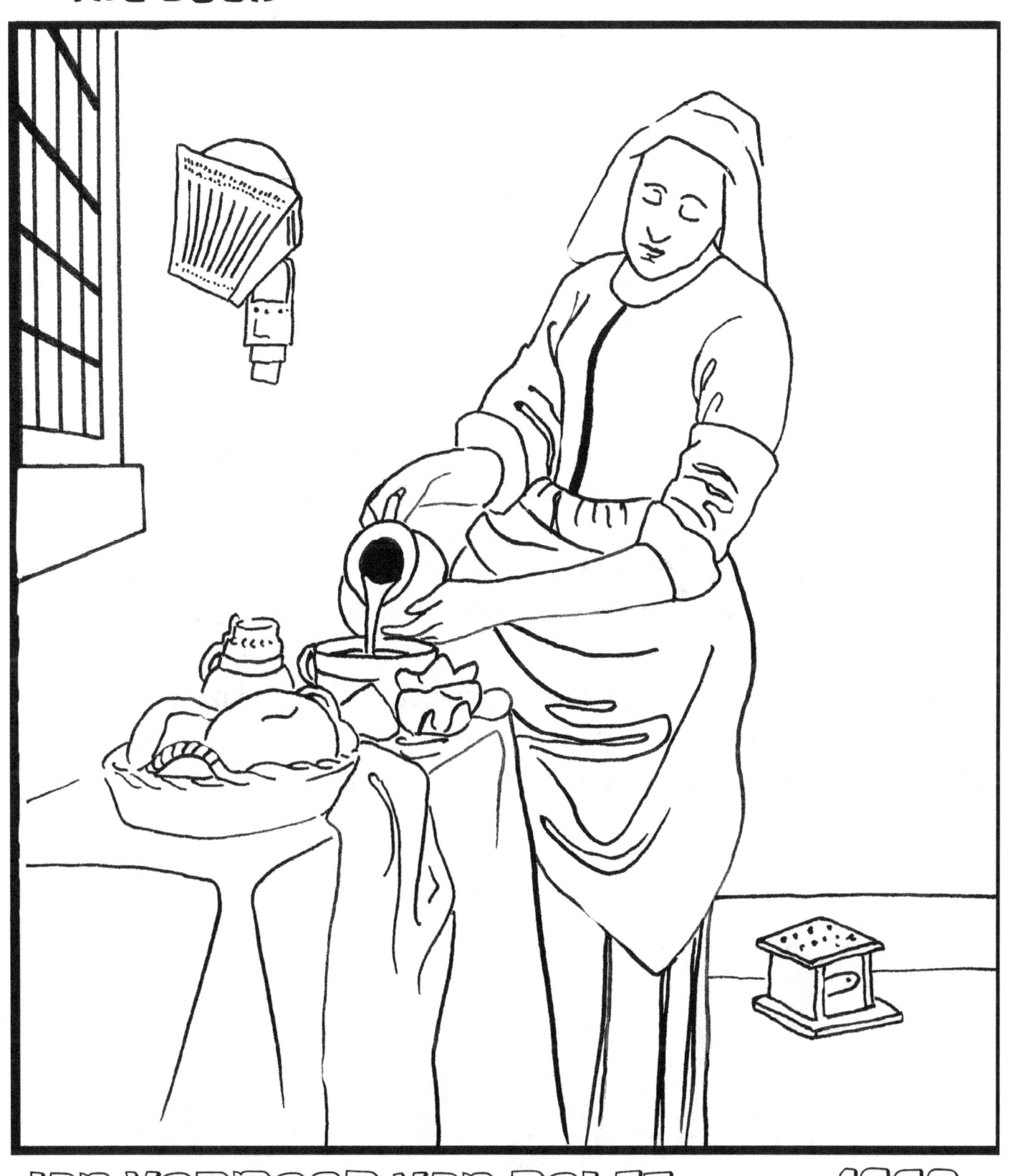

Jan Vermeer van Delft   1660

Jan Vermeer van Delft, 1632-1675

Young Woman with a Water Jug, 1663
Oil on canvas

Vermeer's capturing of women and servants has helped costumers and historians to understand the culture of those days more completely. The way he captured light from windows is magical.

The movie *The Girl with the Pearl Earring*, although not really suitable for children to watch, explained possible painting methods and lifestyle habits of Vermeer. He painted with layers of transparent color that could be considered glazing, a method used later by Maxfield Parrish to create his luminous blues and deep reds. Vermeer obviously adopted the philosophy of Da Vinci that all objects share reflections of colors from objects adjacent to them. He also was one of the few painters of the time to be so lavish as to use real lapis lazuli, a semi-precious stone from Egypt used in blue paint. Because this was so expensive, it is suggested that he must have had a patron who supplied it.

YOUNG WOMAN WITH A WATER JUG

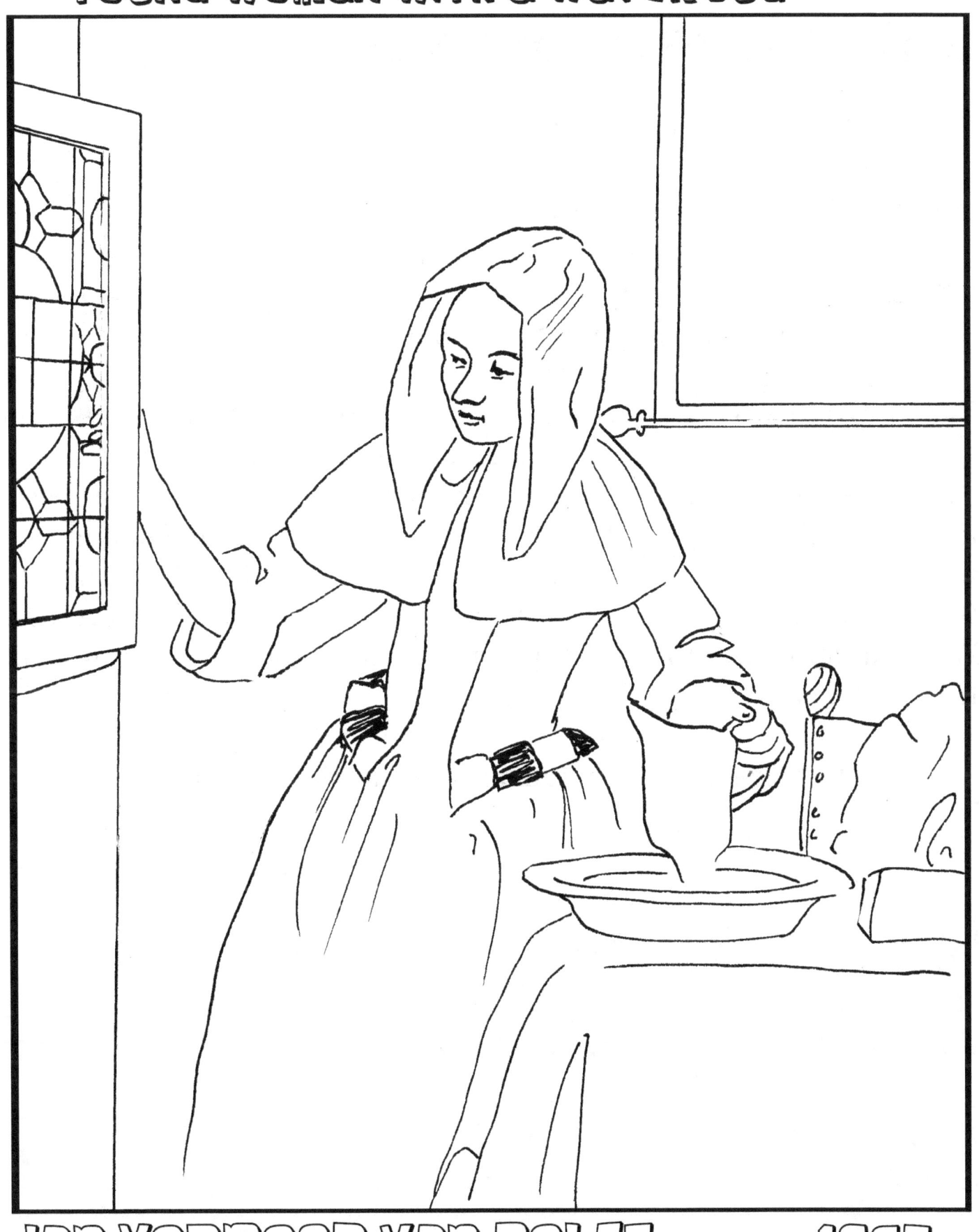

Jan Vermeer van Delft   1663

Benjamin West, 1738-1820

The Death of General Wolfe, 1770

Benjamin West was one of the most influential painters of the American Colonial artistic movement. He began his career as a portrait artist but soon became intrigued with historical painting. His work helped influence the neoclassical movement of the day.

The 10th child of a Pennsylvania Innkeeper, West was mostly self-taught. A friend included him in a group of Pennsylvanians who took a three-year trip to Italy to study art and copy the Italian Renaissance masters, such as Titian and Raphael. In 1763 he moved to London where he remained the rest of his life. His painting of the Death of General Wolfe was so well received that he was obliged to paint copies. West was appointed the official painter of King George III at an annual fee of a thousand pounds.

Later in life, he dabbled with Romanticism and influenced Delacroix.

The Death of General Wolfe

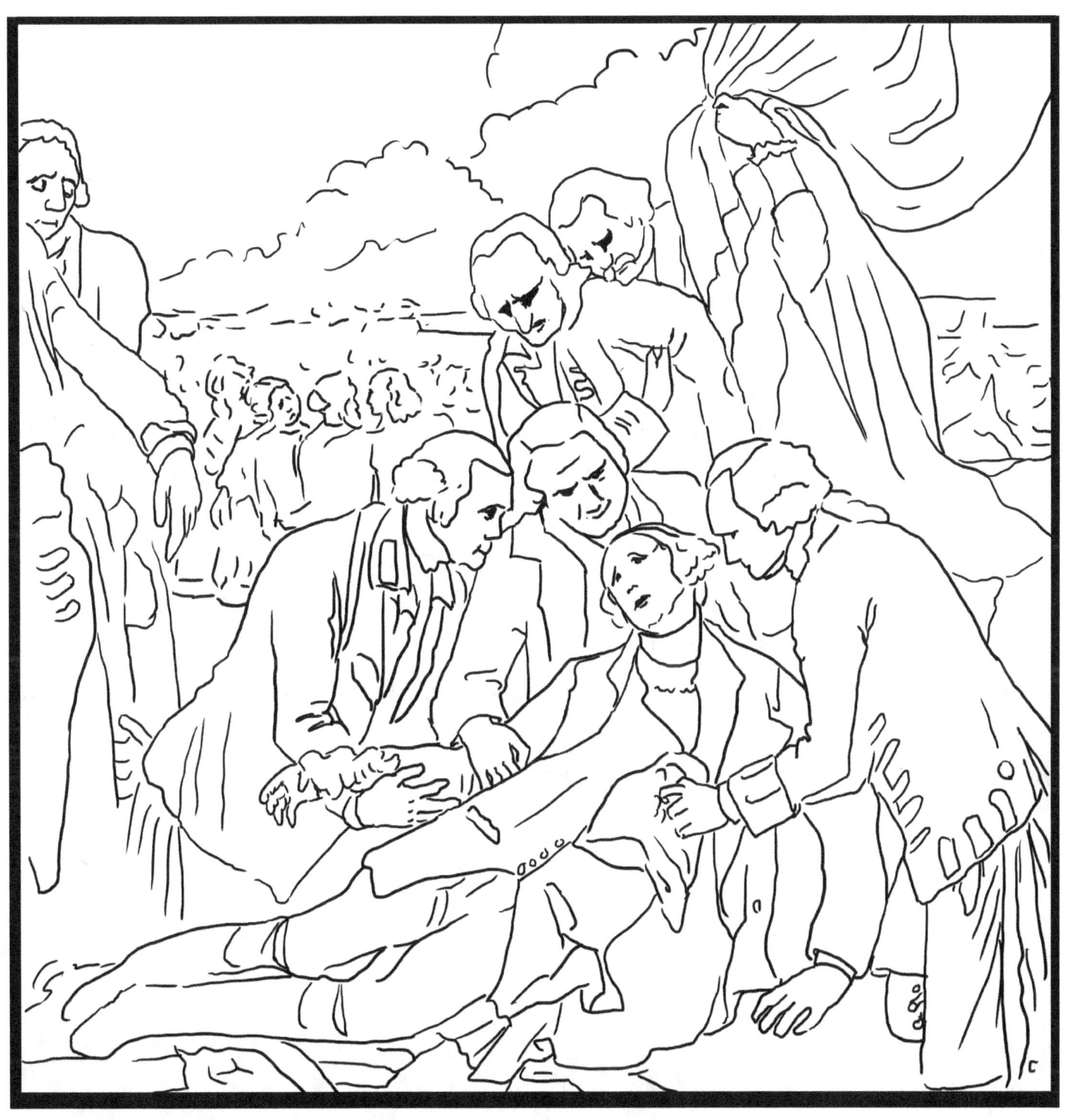

Benjamin West

1770

Thomas Gainsborough, 1727-1788

Blue Boy, 1774

Gainsborough was one of the most famous portrait painters of the British 18th century. His father, a weaver by trade, was impressed with his son's penciling skills and let him go to London to study art at the age of 13. He began painting landscapes, which didn't sell well and switched to painting portraits, first of squires and merchants. As his fame and skill improved he began painting portraits for a higher society clientele, until finally painting the portrait of King George III and his queen. Afterwards he received many more royal commissions. His only known assistant was his nephew, Gainsborough Dupont.

Experts examining the Blue Boy discovered some brush strokes that did not make sense to the picture so the painting was x-rayed. They discovered that under the "rock" at the right of Blue Boy's feet was originally painted a little dog. Perhaps Gainsborough thought the little dog took away from the composition. For whatever reason, he painted over it and left just a brown rock where there was a little dog.

BLUE BOY

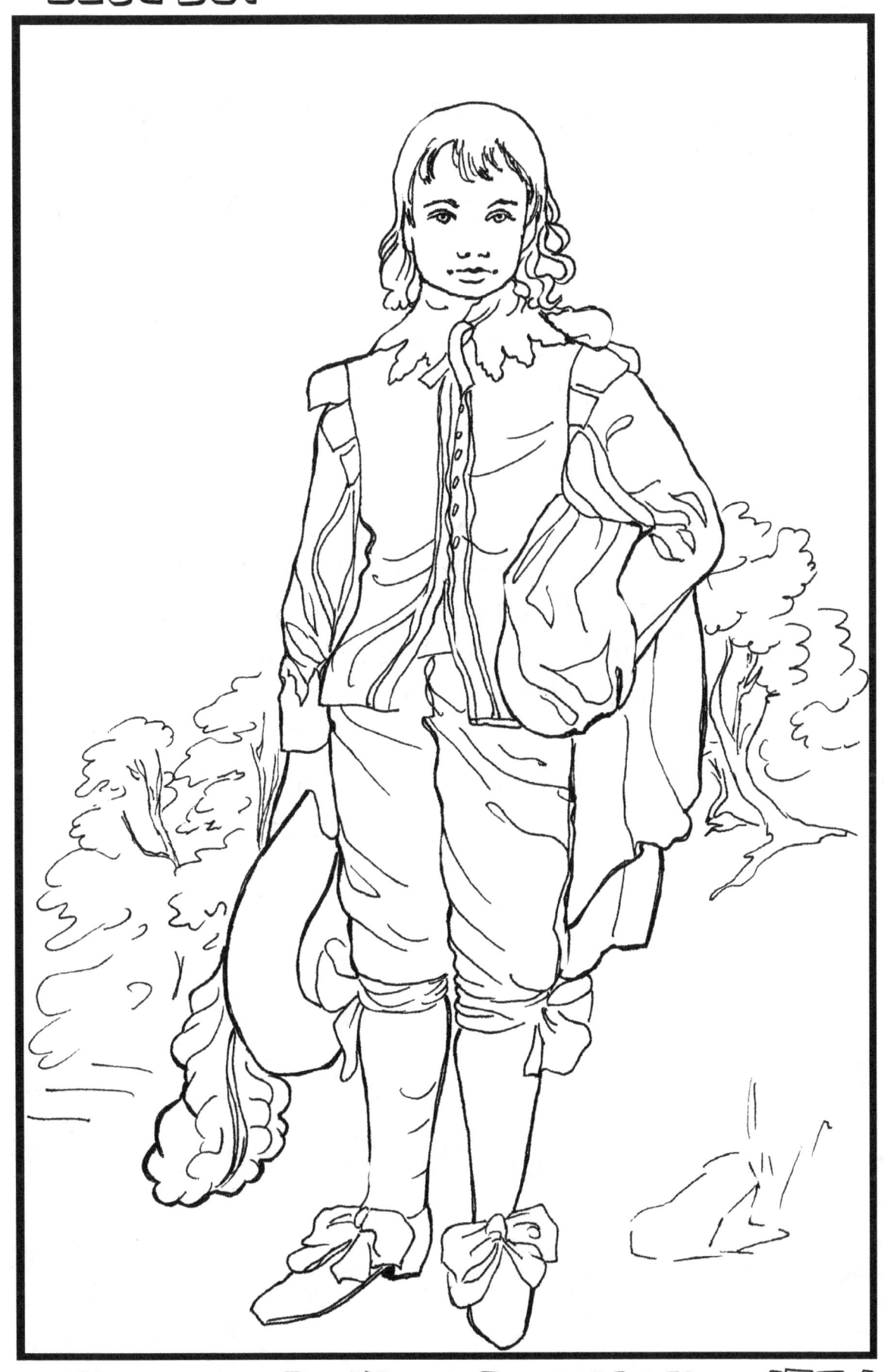

THOMAS GAINSBOROUGH   1774

SIR JOSHUA REYNOLDS, 1723-1792

Portrait of Miss Bowles with Her Dog, 1775

Like Gainsborough, Reynolds was one of the foremost painters in England. He would have loved nothing more than to paint history pictures, but in order to make a living (like most artists) he was forced to paint portraits to earn money.

After studying the effects of Tintoretto and Titian in Rome, Reynolds tried using transparent glazes over a monochrome under-painting. Unfortunately the pigment he chose for the flesh colors was not permanent and even during his lifetime began to fade. This explains the overly pale faces in many of his portraits.

"A room hung with pictures is a room hung with thoughts."
Sir Joshua Reynolds

PORTRAIT OF MISS BOWLES WITH HER DOG

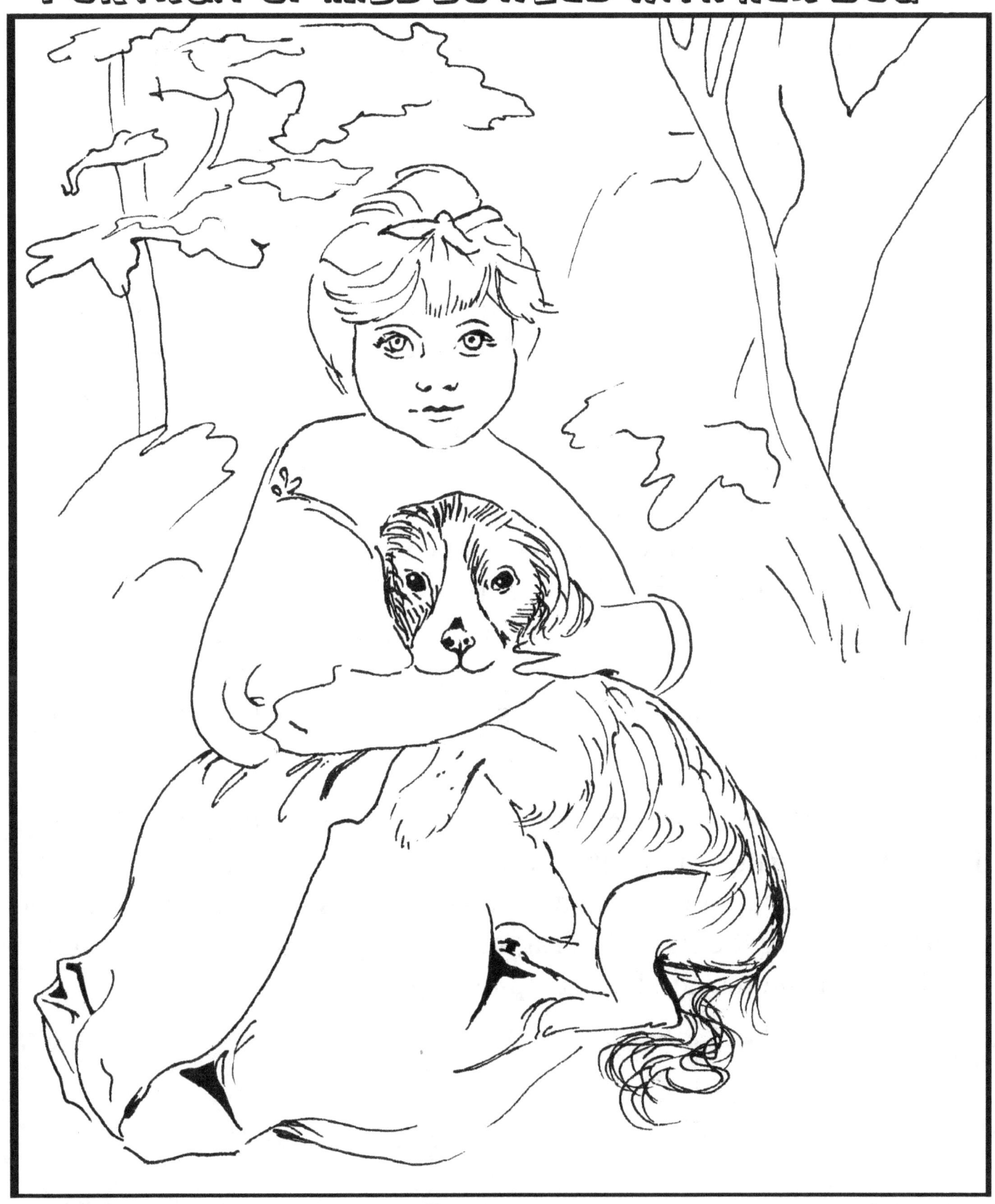

SIR JOSHUA REYNOLDS   1775

Jean-Honoré Fragonard, 1732-1806

A Young Girl Reading, 1776

Oil on canvas

Fragonard painting in a Rococo manner, was one of the most prolific artists of the last decade of the Ancien Régime. He was known for conveying an atmosphere of intimacy, as if peeking into the inner rooms of a home. He studied under several luminists of the day before going to Rome to study. He admired the masters of the Dutch and Flemish schools and imitated their loose brush stokes. It was the wealthy patrons of the Louis XV's court who turned him toward scenes of love and voluptuousness, with which his name shall ever be associated. The French Revolution deprived him of his more wealthy private patrons, either because of exile or the guillotine. He found it wise to leave Paris and lived for some years with his cousin in Grasse. He later returned to Paris and died virtually forgotten.

A Young Girl Reading is from a series of paintings of simple solitude, not meant to be portraits but more of a fantasy portrait. It was said by his friends that he could paint a portrait like this in an hour, using bold colors and energetic strokes. Fragonard enjoyed blurring the distinction between sketch and finished painting.

A YOUNG GIRL READING

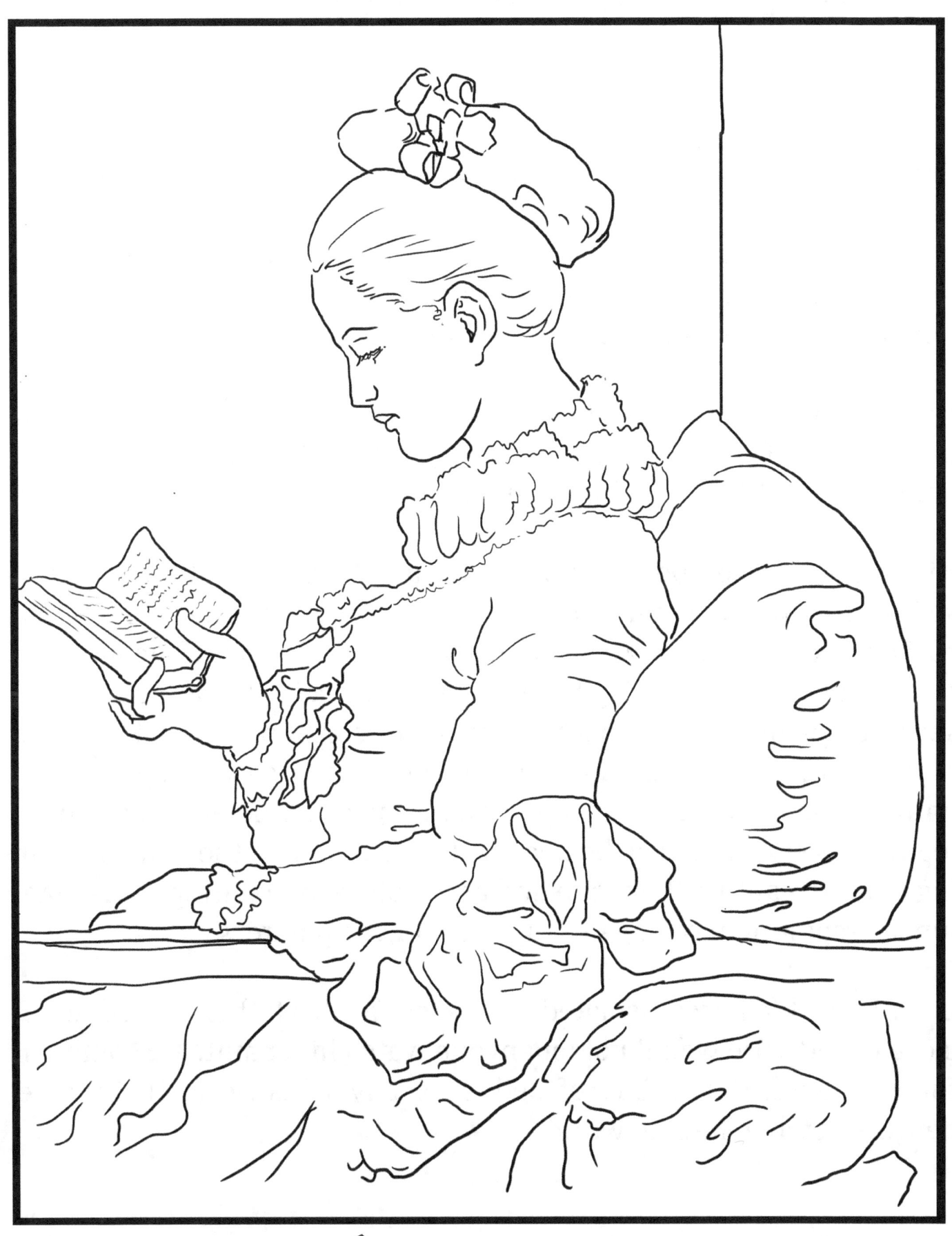

JEAN-HONORÉ FRAGONARD   1776

J. M. W. TURNER, (1775-1851)

Dutch Boats in a Gale, 1801

Born John Mallord William Turner, the English born painter was the leading landscape painter of the day producing a large number of both oil and watercolor paintings. It was his unique combination of Romanticism and realism that had significant influence on the contemporaries of England, France and America.

He was commonly known as the "Painter of Light," a title which is now passed on to Thomas Kincaid, he is regarded as the best landscape painter in the history of European painting.

His father was a barber and wig maker, and by the age of 13 he was selling drawings and paintings in the window of his father's shop. His early works were all in watercolor. By the time he was 18 he had his own studio and was selling both oil and watercolor landscape and seascape paintings. This early success allowed him financial freedom to travel through France, Switzerland, and Italy. He was inspired by natural disasters and catastrophes, painting fires, violent seas and fog. As his style matured he became less involved in the details, desiring more to capture the mood and atmosphere of painting. This made him a great influence on later Impressionistic painters.

Later in his life he was isolated and except for his father, he had no close friends. He would not let anyone watch him paint. He sometimes held exhibitions but refused to sell any of his work. He became depressed when he sold work.

DUTCH BOATS IN A GALE

J. M. W. TURNER

1801

Katsushika Hokusai, 1760-1849

The Great Wave off Kanagawa, 1830-1833

Woodblock print, Museum of Fine Arts, Boston MA, USA

The Great Wave was one of a series called Thirty-six Views of Mount Fuji, but became the best known of the series, both in Japan and in other countries. The significant thing about Japanese wood block prints is that it so profoundly affected the Impressionist movement a world away in France.

Hokusai was known by many different names during his lifetime, which was normal for Japanese artists and helps to divide his work into periods. When he left the traditional studio doing block prints of actors and courtesans, and began doing everyday life and landscapes, his fame was set.

The Great Wave off Kanagawa

1829-1832

Katsushika Hokusai

REMBRANDT PEALE, 1778-1860

Portrait of George Washington, 1840

Oil on Canvas

Rembrandt Peale, an American artist and museum keeper, whose father was the forerunner of a number of American Peale artists. Rembrandt Peale is responsible for painting the likeness of presidents George Washington and Thomas Jefferson, along with famous portraits of American personalities including James Calhoun and Chief Justice John Marshall. He studied art in Paris and was influenced by the Neo-Classical movement. His father was also a notable artist and, of course, named him after the revered Dutch Painter, Rembrandt van Rijn. His father taught all his sons, including Raphaelle Peale and Rubens Peale, to paint scenery and portraiture. It was Washington who most fascinated Rembrandt, though. After first meeting him at the age of 17, he painted him again and again, trying to master the likeness. He turned out over 70 detailed replicas of Washington from artists such as Gilbert Stuart ((including the portrait found on the dollar bill), some in full military uniform, one of which hangs in the Oval Office today.

PORTRAITE OF GEORGE WASHINGTON

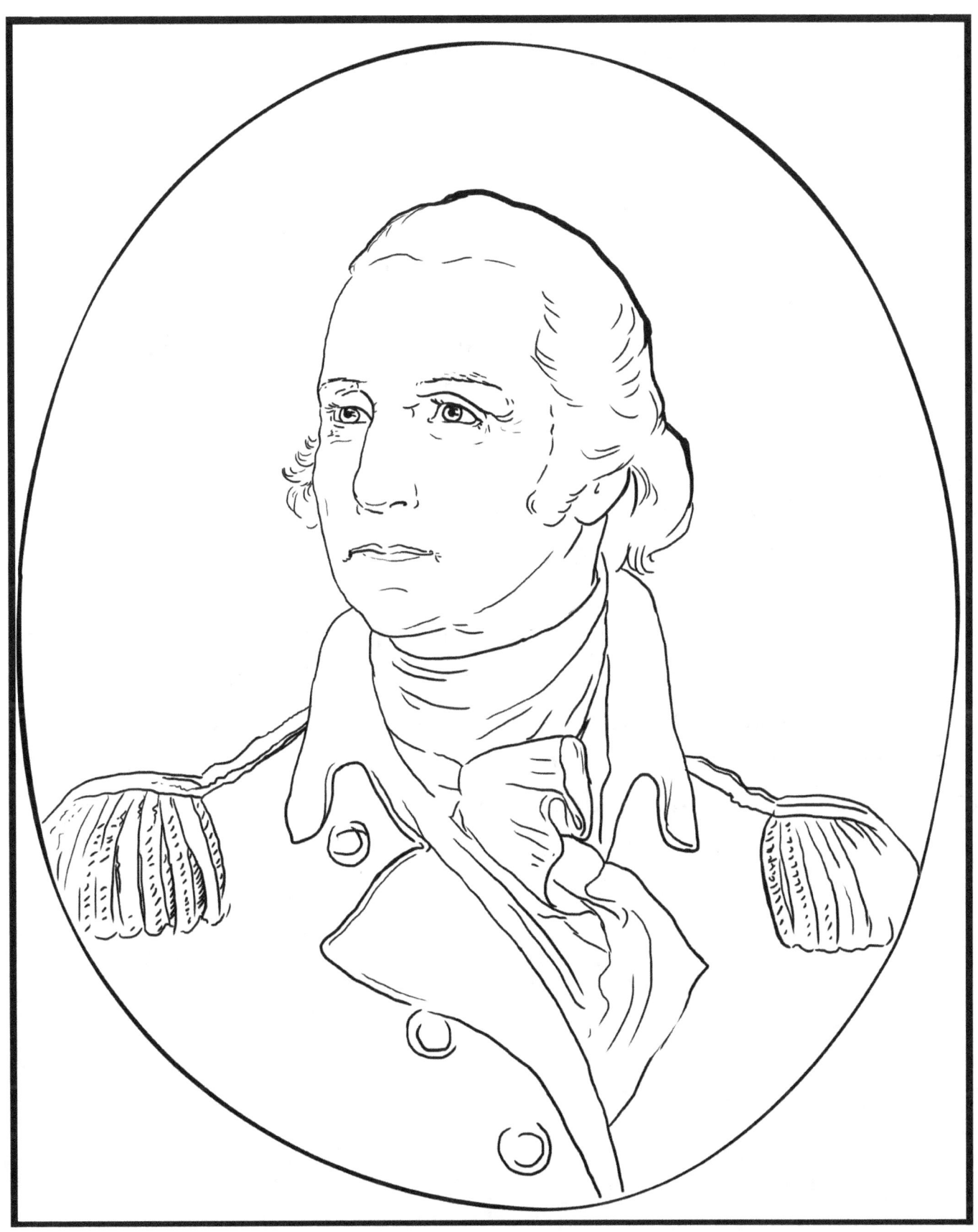

REMBRANDT PEALE   1840

J. M. W. TURNER, (1775-1851)

The Bell Rock Lighthouse, 1824

Born John Mallord William Turner, the English born painter was the leading landscape painter of the day producing a large number of both oil and watercolor paintings. It was his unique combination of Romanticism and realism that had significant influence on the contemporaries of England, France and America.

He was commonly known as the "Painter of Light," a title which is now passed on to Thomas Kincaid, he is regarded as the best landscape painter in the history of European painting.

This is a painting of a stormy turbulent sea swamping the schooner, which is perilously close to shore, just beyond the lighthouse. Turner has a way with painting disasters just before the climactic moment. It is a breathtaking painting. Another in a long line of enchanting disasters that Turner loved to paint.

THE BELL ROCK LIGHTHOUSE

J.M.W. TURNER

1824

eugene DeLacroix, 1798-1863

Arab Rider Attacked by a Lion, 1849-1850

Oil on panel, Potter Palmer Collection

Born Ferdinand Victor Eugene Delacroix, he was a member of the Romanticism movement of art. Rubens and the Venetian Renaissance painters, and their approach to color and movement rather than a carefully rendered form inspired him. Baudelaire said of him, "Delacroix was passionately in love with passion, but coldly determined to express passion as clearly as possible."

"A man throws himself out of the fourth-floor window: if you can't make a sketch of him before he gets to the ground, you will never do anything big."

Eugene Delacroix

ARAB RIDER ATTACKED BY LION

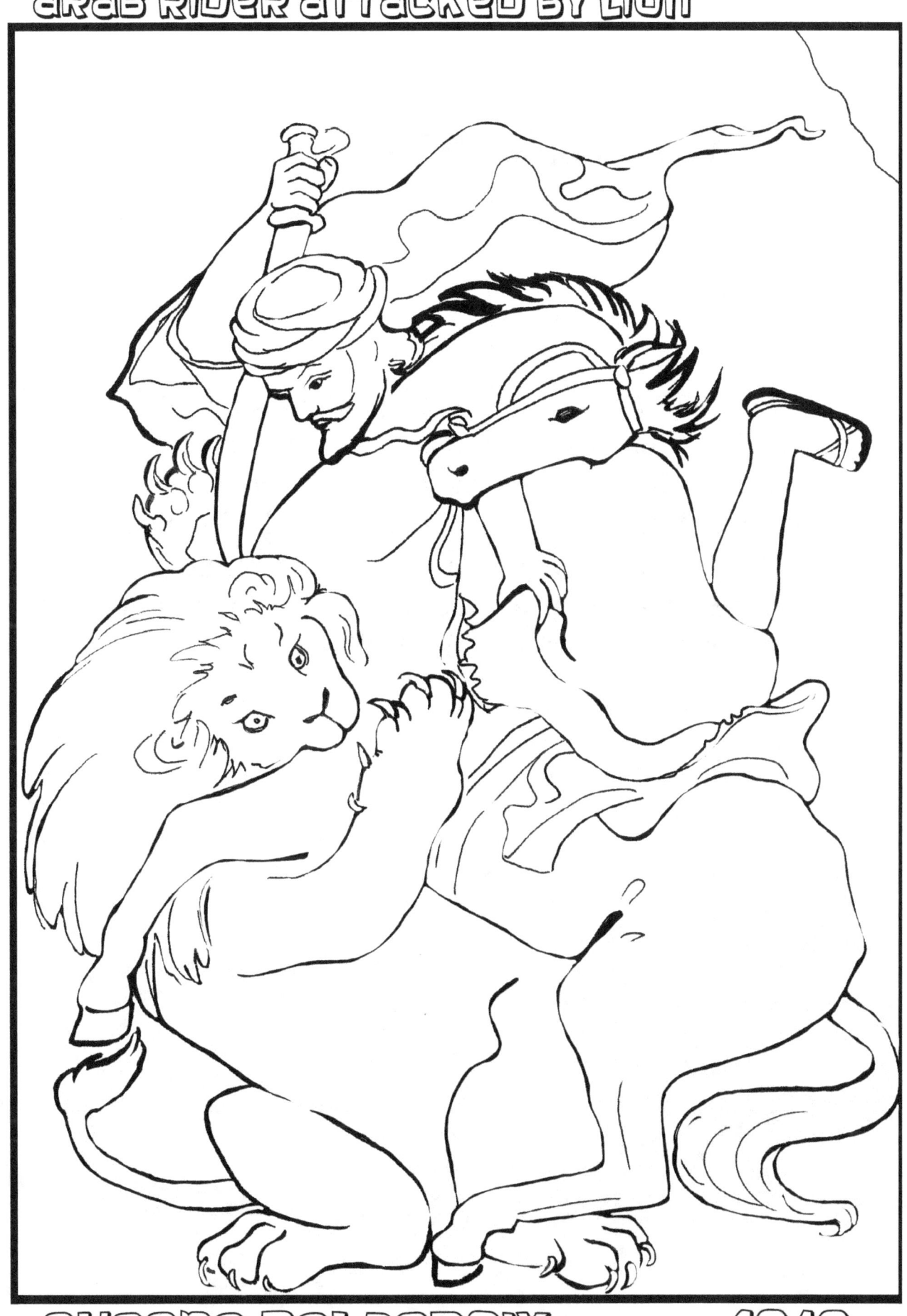

EUGENE DELACROIX   1849

Léon Bonvin, 1834-1866

The Cook, 1862
Watercolor

Bonvin was born in a Parisian suburb and had artistic ambitions from
an early age. It was his brother François who achieved some measure
of success. Léon was largely self-taught, studying the Dutch masters
style. He painted from nature and scenes from the Inn he managed.
He decided to take his watercolors to an art dealer and after being
turned down, he hanged himself in the forest of Meudon. The later
sale of his watercolors raised over 8,000 francs for his destitute family.

THE COOK

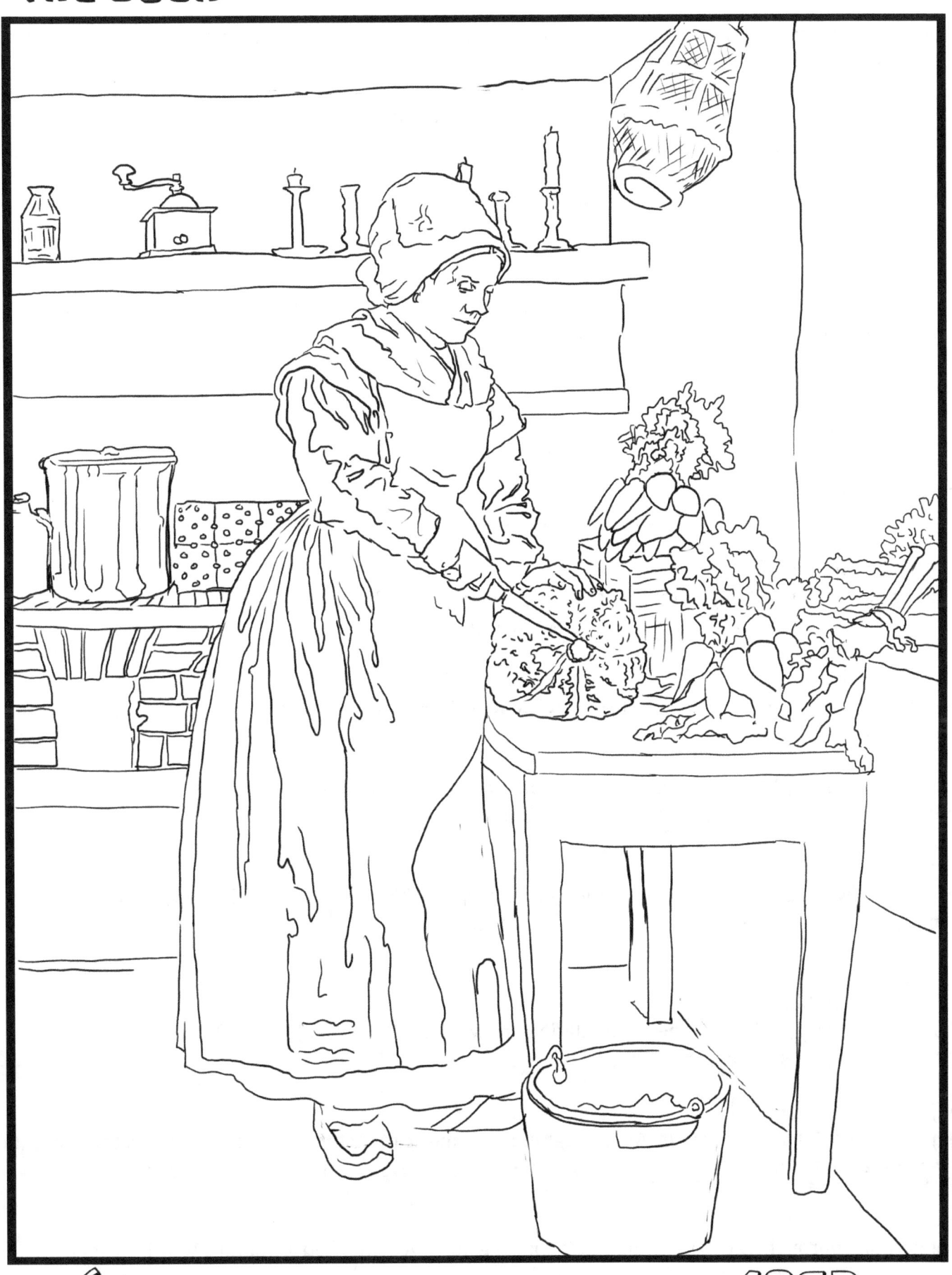

Léon Bonvin   1862

REFERENCES

Healey, Deryck. Living with Color, The Workbook for Managing the Colors in Your Home, Rand McNally & Co., Chicago IL, 1982, Print.

Color Wheel Pro: Color Meaning. (2013). Color meaning website. Retrieved Jul 22, 2014 from www.color-wheel-pro.com/color-meaning.html

Norris, Stephanie. Secrets of Color Healing, DK Publishing, Inc., New York, Print, 2001, pg 62.

Hume, Helen D. (1998). The Art Teacher's Book of Lists, New Jersey, Prentice Hall, Pgs 46-47, print.

Art History. (2014). Art History.com. website. Retrieved July 20, 2013 from http://arthistory.about.com/cs/reference/a/art_history_one_3.htm

El Greco
El Greco. (2014). The Biography.com website. Retrieved 09:54, Jul 20, 2014, from http://www.biography.com/people/el-greco-9319123.

Georges de Latour
http://www.abcgallery.com/L/latour/latourbio.html

Rembrandt van Rijn
Rembrandt Van Rijn. (2014). Rembrandt Painting.net website. Retrieved Jul 21, 2014 from http://www.rembrandtpainting.net/rembrandt_life_and_work.htm

Peter Paul Rubens
Night Scene. (2014). Peter Paul Rubens-Night Scene on Wikipedia website. Retrieved Jul 22, 2014 from http://fr.wikipedia.org/wiki/Fichier:Peter_Paul_Rubens_-_Night_Scene_-_WGA20423.jpg

Peter Paul Rubens. (2014). Peter Paul Rubens biography on Wikipedia website. Reteieved Jul 22, 2014 from http://en.wikipedia.org/wiki/Peter_Paul_Rubens

Sir Anthony van Dyck
Antoon van Dyck. (2014). Anthony van Dyck biography on Wikipedia website. Retrieved Jul 22, 2014 from http://www.wikipedia.org/wiki/Anthony_van_Dyck

Jan Vermeer van Delft
Johannes Vermeer. (2014). Vermeer Foundation.org website. Retrieved Jul 21, 2014 from http://www.vermeer-foundation.org/biography.html

Benjamin West
Benjamin West. (2014). Benjamin West; Biography of American History Painter & Portraitist website. Retrieved Jul 21, 2014 from http://www.visual-arts-cork.com/famous-artists/benjamin-west.htm

Thomas Gainsborough
Thomas Gainsborough. (2014). Thomas Gainsborough.org website. Retrieved Jul 21, 2014 from http://www.thomas-gainsborough.org/biography.html

Sir Joshua Reynolds
Joshua Reynolds. (2014). Sir Joshua Reynolds; Encyclopedia Britannica website. Retrieved Jul 21, 2014 from http://www.britannica.com/EBchecked/topic/500800/Sir-Joshua-Reynolds/6138/Later-years

Jean-Honoré Fragonard
Jean-Honoré Fragonard. (2014). Biography on Wikipedia.org website. Retrieved Jul 21, 2014 from http://en.wikipedia.org/wiki/Jean-Honor%C3%A9_Fragonard

A Young Girl Reading. (2014). The Collection; National Gallery of Art website. Retrieved Jul 21, 2014 from http://www.nga.gov/collection/gallery/gg55/gg55-46303.html

JMW Turner
JMW Turner. (2014). Biography on Wikipedia.org website. Retrieved Jul 21, 2014 from http://en.wikipedia.org/wiki/J._M._W._Turner

JMW Turner. (2014). JMW Turner; Biography and Paintings of English Landscape Artist, Watercolour Painter website. Retrieved Jul 21, 2014 from http://www.visual-arts-cork.com/famous-artists/turner.htm

Hokusai
Katsushika Hokusai. (2014). Katsushika Hokusai.org website. Retrieved Jul 21, 2014 from http://www.katsushikahokusai.org/

Katsushika Hokusai. (2014). Katsushika Hokusai biography on Wikipedia.org website. Retrieved Jul 21, 2014 from http://en.wikipedia.org/wiki/Hokusai

Hokusai, by Gian Carlo Calza, Phaidon Press, 2004, print.

Rembrandt Peale
Rembrandt Peale. (2014). Rembrandt Peale biography on Wikipedia website. Retrieved Jul 22, 2014 from http://en.wikipedia.org/wiki/Rembrandt_Peale

Eugene Delacroix
Delacroix. (2014). Eugene Delacroix biography on Wikipedia website. Retrieved Jul 22, 2014 from http://en.wikipedia.org/wiki/Eug%C3%A8ne_Delacroix
Jobert, Barthelemy. Delacroix, Princeton University Press, 1998, print.

Léon Bonvin
Léon Bonvin. (2014). The J. Paul Getty Museum; Artists website. Retrieved Jul 21, 2014 from http://www.getty.edu/art/gettyguide/artMakerDetails?maker=3486

BIBLIOGRAPHY

Healey, Deryck. Living with Color, The Workbook for Managing the Colors in Your Home, Rand McNally & Co., Chicago IL, 1982, Print.

Norris, Stephanie. Secrets of Color Healing, DK Publishing, Inc., New York, Print, 2001, pg 62.

Georges de La Tour. by I. Nemilova. Leningrad-Moscow. 1958.

Georges de La Tour. by Yu. Zolotov. Moscow. 1979.

Hokusai, by Gian Carlo Calza, Phaidon Press, 2004, print.

Delacroix, by Barthelemy Jobert, Princeton University Press, 1998, print.

Hume, Helen D. (1998). The Art Teacher's Book of Lists, New Jersey, Prentice Hall, print.

www.ingramcontent.com/pod-product-compliance
Lightning Source LLC
Chambersburg PA
CBHW081231170526
45165CB00009B/3031